MYSTERIUM FIDEI

MYSTERIUM FIDEI

ENCYCLICAL ON THE HOLY EUCHARIST

POPE PAUL VI

Our Sunday Visitor
Huntington, Indiana

Published by Our Sunday Visitor, Inc., in 2023

28 27 26 25 24 23 1 2 3 4 5 6 7 8 9

Our Sunday Visitor Publishing Division
Our Sunday Visitor, Inc.
200 Noll Plaza
Huntington, IN 46750
1-800-348-2440

ISBN: 978-1-63966-200-5 (Inventory No. T2895)

Cover design: Tyler Ottinger
Cover art: Adobe Stock
Interior design: Amanda Falk

PRINTED IN THE UNITED STATES OF AMERICA

To his venerable Brothers the patriarchs, primates, archbishops, bishops, and other local ordinaries in peace and communion with the apostolic see, and to the clergy and faithful of the entire world.

Venerable Brothers and Dear Sons, Health and Apostolic Benediction.

1. The Mystery of Faith, that is, the ineffable gift of the Eucharist that the Catholic Church received from Christ, her Spouse, as a pledge of his immense love, is something that she has always devoutly guarded as her most precious treasure, and during the Second Vatican Council she professed her faith and veneration in a new and solemn declaration. In dealing with the restoration of the sacred liturgy, the fathers of the council were led by their pastoral concern for the whole Church to regard it as a matter of highest importance to urge the faithful to participate actively, with undivided faith and the utmost devotion, in the celebration of this Most Holy Mystery, to offer it to God along with the priest as a sacrifice for their own salvation and that of the whole world, and to use it as spiritual nourishment.

2. For if the sacred liturgy holds first place in the life of the Church, then the Eucharistic Mystery stands at the heart and center of the liturgy, since it is the font of life that cleanses us and strengthens us to live not for ourselves but for God and to be united to each other by the closest ties of love.

Reaffirmation by Vatican II

3. In order to make the indissoluble bond that exists between faith and devotion perfectly clear, the fathers of the council decided, in the course of reaffirming the doctrine that the Church has always held and taught and that was solemnly defined by the Council of Trent, to offer the following compendium of truths as an introduction to their treatment of the Most Holy Mystery of the Eucharist:

4. "At the Last Supper, on the night when he was betrayed, our Savior instituted the Eucharistic Sacrifice of his body and blood. He did this in order to perpetuate the Sacrifice of the Cross throughout the centuries until he should come again, and so to entrust to his beloved spouse, the Church, a memorial of his death and resurrection: a sacrament of love, a sign

of unity, a bond of charity, a paschal banquet in which Christ is eaten, the mind is filled with grace, and a pledge of future glory is given to us."[1]

Both Sacrifice and Sacrament Highlighted

5. These words highlight both the sacrifice, which pertains to the essence of the Mass that is celebrated daily, and the sacrament in which those who participate in it through holy Communion eat the flesh of Christ and drink the blood of Christ, and thus receive grace, which is the beginning of eternal life, and the "medicine of immortality" according to Our Lord's words: "The man who eats my flesh and drinks my blood enjoys eternal life, and I will raise him up on the last day."[2]

Restoration of Liturgy Linked to Eucharistic Devotion

6. And so we earnestly hope that the restoration of the Sacred Liturgy will produce abundant fruits in the form of Eucharistic devotion, so that the holy Church may, with this salvific sign of piety raised on high, make daily progress

toward the full achievement of unity,[3] inviting all Christians to a unity of faith and love and drawing them to it gently, through the action of divine grace.

7. We seem to have a preview of these fruits and a first taste of them in the outpouring of joy and eagerness that has marked the reception the sons of the Catholic Church have accorded to the Constitution on the Sacred Liturgy and to the restoration of the liturgy; and we find these fruits, too, in the large number of carefully edited publications that make it their purpose to go into the doctrine of the holy Eucharist more profoundly and to come to a more fruitful understanding of it, especially in terms of its relationship to the mystery of the Church.

8. All of this brings us deep consolation and joy. And it gives us great pleasure to inform you of this, venerable brothers, so that you may join with us in giving thanks to God, the bestower of all gifts, who rules the Church and makes her grow in virtue through his Spirit.

REASONS FOR PASTORAL CONCERN AND ANXIETY

9. There are, however, venerable brothers, a number of reasons for serious pastoral concern and anxiety in this very matter that we are now discussing, and because of our consciousness of our apostolic office, we cannot remain silent about them.

False and Disturbing Opinions

10. For we can see that some of those who are dealing with this Most Holy Mystery in speech and writing are disseminating opinions on Masses celebrated in private or on the dogma of transubstantiation that are disturbing the minds of the faithful and causing them no small measure of confusion about matters of faith, just as if it were all right for someone to take doctrine that has already been defined by the Church and consign it to oblivion, or else interpret it in such a way as to weaken the genuine meaning of the words or the recognized force of the concepts involved.

11. To give an example of what we are talking about, it is not permissible to extol the so-called community Mass in such a way as to detract from Masses that are

celebrated privately; or to concentrate on the notion of sacramental sign as if the symbolism — which no one will deny is certainly present in the most blessed Eucharist — fully expressed and exhausted the manner of Christ's presence in this Sacrament; or to discuss the mystery of transubstantiation without mentioning what the Council of Trent had to say about the marvelous conversion of the whole substance of the bread into the body and the whole substance of the wine into the blood of Christ, as if they involve nothing more than "transignification," or "transfinalization," as they call it; or, finally, to propose and act upon the opinion that Christ, Our Lord, is no longer present in the consecrated Hosts that remain after the celebration of the sacrifice of the Mass has been completed.

12. Everyone can see that the spread of these and similar opinions does great harm to belief in and devotion to the Eucharist.

Purpose of the Encyclical

13. And so, with the aim of seeing to it that the hope to which the council has

given rise — that a new wave of Eucharistic devotion will sweep over the Church — not be reduced to nil through the sowing of the seeds of false opinions, we have decided to use our apostolic authority and speak our mind to you on this subject, venerable brothers.

14. We certainly do not deny that those who are spreading these strange opinions are making a praiseworthy effort to investigate this lofty Mystery and to set forth its inexhaustible riches and to make it more understandable to the men of today; rather, we acknowledge this, and we approve of it. But we cannot approve the opinions that they set forth, and we have an obligation to warn you about the grave danger that these opinions involve for true faith.

HOLY EUCHARIST A MYSTERY OF FAITH

15. First of all, we want to recall something that you know very well but that is absolutely necessary if the virus of every kind of rationalism is to be repelled; it is something that many illustrious martyrs have witnessed to with their blood, some-

thing that celebrated Fathers and Doctors of the Church have constantly professed and taught. We mean the fact that the Eucharist is a very great mystery — in fact, properly speaking, and in the words of the Sacred Liturgy, the Mystery of Faith. "It contains within it," as Leo XIII, our predecessor of happy memory, very wisely remarked, "all supernatural realities in a remarkable richness and variety of miracles."[4]

Relying on Revelation, Not Reason

16. And so we must approach this mystery in particular with humility and reverence, not relying on human reasoning, which ought to hold its peace, but rather adhering firmly to divine revelation.

17. St. John Chrysostom who, as you know, dealt with the Mystery of the Eucharist in such eloquent language and with such insight born of devotion, had these most fitting words to offer on one occasion when he was instructing his faithful about this mystery: "Let us submit to God in all things and not contradict him, even if what he says seems to contradict our reason and intellect; let his word prevail

over our reason and intellect. Let us act in this way with regard to the Eucharistic mysteries, and not limit our attention just to what can be perceived by the senses, but instead hold fast to his words. For his word cannot deceive."[5]

18. The scholastic Doctors [of the Church] made similar statements on more than one occasion. As St. Thomas says, the fact that the true body and the true blood of Christ are present in this Sacrament "cannot be apprehended by the senses but only by faith, which rests upon divine authority. This is why Cyril comments upon the words, 'This is my body which is delivered up for you' in Luke 22:19, in this way: 'Do not doubt that this is true; instead accept the words of the Savior in faith; for since He is truth, He cannot tell a lie.'"[6]

19. Hence the Christian people often follow the lead of St. Thomas and sing the words: "Sight, touch, and taste in thee are each deceived; / The ear alone most safely is believed. / I believe all the Son of God has spoken; / Than truth's own word, there is no truer token."

20. And St. Bonaventure declares: "There is no difficulty over Christ's being present in the Sacrament as in a sign; the great difficulty is in the fact that he is really in the Sacrament, as he is in heaven. And so believing this is especially meritorious."[7]

Example of the Apostles

21. Moreover, the holy Gospel alludes to this when it tells of the many disciples of Christ who turned away and left Our Lord after hearing him speak of eating his flesh and drinking his blood. "This is strange talk," they said. "Who can be expected to listen to it." Peter, on the contrary, replied to Jesus' question as to whether the Twelve wanted to go away, too, by promptly and firmly expressing his own faith and that of the other apostles in these marvelous words: "Lord, to whom should we go? Thy words are the words of eternal life."[8]

22. It is only logical, then, for us to follow the magisterium of the Church as a guiding star in carrying on our investigations into this mystery, for the Divine Redeemer has entrusted the safeguarding and the explanation of the written or transmitted word of God to her. And we are convinced

that "whatever has been preached and believed throughout the whole Church with true Catholic faith since the days of antiquity is true, even if it not be subject to rational investigation, and even if it not be explained in words."[9]

Proper Wording of Great Importance

23. But this is not enough. Once the integrity of the Faith has been safeguarded, then it is time to guard the proper way of expressing it, lest our careless use of words give rise, God forbid, to false opinions regarding faith in the most sublime things. St. Augustine gives a stern warning about this when he takes up the matter of the different ways of speaking that are employed by the philosophers on the one hand and that ought to be used by Christians on the other. "The philosophers," he says, "use words freely, and they have no fear of offending religious listeners in dealing with subjects that are difficult to understand. But we have to speak in accordance with a fixed rule, so that a lack of restraint in speech on our part may not give rise to some irreverent opinion about the things represented by the words."[10]

24. And so the rule of language which the Church has established through the long labor of centuries, with the help of the Holy Spirit, and which she has confirmed with the authority of the councils, and which has more than once been the watchword and banner of orthodox faith, is to be religiously preserved, and no one may presume to change it at his own pleasure or under the pretext of new knowledge. Who would ever tolerate that the dogmatic formulas used by the ecumenical councils for the mysteries of the Holy Trinity and the Incarnation be judged as no longer appropriate for men of our times, and let others be rashly substituted for them? In the same way, it cannot be tolerated that any individual should on his own authority take something away from the formulas which were used by the Council of Trent to propose the Eucharistic Mystery for our belief. These formulas — like the others that the Church used to propose the dogmas of faith — express concepts that are not tied to a certain specific form of human culture, or to a certain level of scientific progress, or to one or another theological school. Instead, they set forth what the

human mind grasps of reality through necessary and universal experience and what it expresses in apt and exact words, whether it be in ordinary or more refined language. For this reason, these formulas are adapted to all men of all times and all places.

Greater Clarity of Expression Always Possible

25. They can, it is true, be made clearer and more obvious; and doing this is of great benefit. But it must always be done in such a way that they retain the meaning in which they have been used, so that with the advance of an understanding of the Faith, the truth of faith will remain unchanged. For it is the teaching of the First Vatican Council that "the meaning that Holy Mother the Church has once declared, is to be retained forever, and no pretext of deeper understanding ever justifies any deviation from that meaning."[11]

EUCHARISTIC MYSTERY IN SACRIFICE OF THE MASS

26. For the joy and edification of everyone, we would like to review with you, venerable brothers, the doctrine on the Mys-

tery of the Eucharist that has been handed down, and that the Catholic Church holds and teaches with unanimity.

Reenactment at Heart of Doctrine

27. It is a good idea to recall at the very outset what may be termed the heart and core of the doctrine, namely that, by means of the Mystery of the Eucharist, the Sacrifice of the Cross which was once carried out on Calvary is reenacted in wonderful fashion and is constantly recalled, and its salvific power is applied to the forgiving of the sins we commit each day.[12]

28. Just as Moses made the Old Testament sacred with the blood of calves,[13] so, too, Christ the Lord took the New Testament, of which he is the mediator, and made it sacred through his own blood, in instituting the mystery of the Eucharist. For, as the Evangelists narrate, at the Last Supper "he took bread, and blessed and broke it, and gave it to them, saying, 'This is my body, given for you; do this for a commemoration of me.' And so with the cup, when supper was ended, 'This cup,' he said, 'is the new testament, in my blood which is to

be shed for you.'"[14] And by bidding the apostles to do this in memory of him, he made clear that he wanted it to be forever repeated. This intention of Christ was faithfully carried out by the primitive Church through her adherence to the teaching of the apostles and through her gatherings to celebrate the Eucharistic Sacrifice. As St. Luke is careful to point out, "They occupied themselves continually with the apostles' teaching, their fellowship in the breaking of bread, and the fixed times of prayer."[15] The faithful used to derive such spiritual fervor from this practice that it was said of them that "there was one heart and soul in all the company of the believers."[16]

New Offering of the New Testament

29. Moreover, the apostle Paul, who faithfully transmitted to us what he had received from the Lord,[17] is clearly speaking of the Eucharistic Sacrifice when he points out that Christians ought not take part in pagan sacrifices, precisely because they have been made partakers of the table of the Lord. "Is not this cup we bless," he says, "a participation in Christ's blood? Is not the bread we break a participation

in Christ's Body? ... To drink the Lord's cup, and yet to drink the cup of evil spirits, to share the Lord's feast, and to share the feast of evil spirits, is impossible for you."[18] Foreshadowed by Malachi,[19] this new oblation of the New Testament has always been offered by the Church, in accordance with the teaching of Our Lord and the apostles, "not only to atone for the sins and punishments and satisfactions of the living faithful and to appeal for their other needs, but also to help those who have died in Christ but have not yet been completely purified."[20]

Offered Also for the Dead

30. We will pass over the other citations and rest content with recalling the testimony offered by St. Cyril of Jerusalem, who wrote the following memorable words for the neophytes whom he was instructing in the Christian faith: "After the spiritual sacrifice, the un-bloody act of worship, has been completed, we bend over this propitiatory offering and beg God to grant peace to all the Churches, to give harmony to the whole world, to bless our rulers, our soldiers, and our companions, to aid the sick and afflicted, and

in general to assist all those who stand in need; we all pray for all these intentions, and we offer this victim for them ... and last of all for our deceased holy forefathers and bishops and for all those who have lived among us. For we have a deep conviction that great help will be afforded those souls for whom prayers are offered while this holy and awesome victim is present." In support of this, this holy Doctor offers the example of a crown made for an emperor in order to win a pardon for some exiles, and he concludes his talk with these words: "In the same fashion, when we offer our prayers to God for the dead, even those who are sinners, we are not just making a crown but instead are offering Christ who was slaughtered for our sins, and thus begging the merciful God to take pity both on them and on ourselves."[21] St. Augustine attests that this custom of offering the "sacrifice which ransomed us" also for the dead was observed in the Church at Rome,[22] and he mentions at the same time that the universal Church observed this custom as something handed down from the Fathers.[23]

The Universal Priesthood

31. But there is something else that we would like to add that is very helpful in shedding light on the mystery of the Church; we mean the fact that the whole Church plays the role of priest and victim along with Christ, offering the sacrifice of the Mass and itself completely offered in it. The Fathers of the Church taught this wondrous doctrine.[24] A few years ago our predecessor of happy memory, Pius XII, explained it.[25] And only recently the Second Vatican Council reiterated it in its Constitution on the Church, in dealing with the people of God.[26] To be sure, the distinction between the universal priesthood and the hierarchical priesthood is something essential and not just a matter of degree, and it has to be maintained in a proper way.[27] Yet we cannot help being filled with an earnest desire to see this teaching explained over and over until it takes deep root in the hearts of the faithful. For it is a most effective means of fostering devotion to the Eucharist, of extolling the dignity of all the faithful, and of spurring them on to reach the heights of sanctity, which means the total and generous offering of oneself to the service of

the Divine Majesty.

No Mass is "Private"

32. It is also only fitting for us to recall the conclusion that can be drawn from this about "the public and social nature of each and every Mass."[28] For each and every Mass is not something private, even if a priest celebrates it privately; instead, it is an act of Christ and of the Church. In offering this sacrifice, the Church learns to offer herself as a sacrifice for all, and she applies the unique and infinite redemptive power of the Sacrifice of the Cross to the salvation of the whole world. For every Mass that is celebrated is being offered not just for the salvation of certain people, but also for the salvation of the whole world. The conclusion from this is that even though active participation by many faithful is of its very nature particularly fitting when Mass is celebrated, still there is no reason to criticize but rather only to approve a Mass that a priest celebrates privately for a good reason in accordance with the regulations and legitimate traditions of the Church, even when only a server to make the responses is present. For such a Mass brings a rich

and abundant treasure of special graces to help the priest himself, the faithful, the whole Church, and the whole world toward salvation — and this same abundance of graces is not gained through mere reception of holy Communion.

33. And so, we recommend from a paternal and solicitous heart that priests, who constitute our greatest joy and our crown in the Lord, be mindful of the power they have received from the bishop who ordained them — the power of offering sacrifice to God and of celebrating Mass for the living and for the dead in the name of the Lord.[29] We recommend that they celebrate Mass daily in a worthy and devout fashion, so that they themselves and the rest of the faithful may enjoy the benefits that flow in such abundance from the Sacrifice of the Cross. In doing so, they will also be making a great contribution toward the salvation of mankind.

CHRIST SACRAMENTALLY PRESENT IN THE SACRIFICE OF THE MASS

34. The few things that we have touched upon concerning the sacrifice of the Mass

encourage us to say something about the Sacrament of the Eucharist, since both Sacrifice and Sacrament pertain to the same mystery and cannot be separated from each other. The Lord is immolated in an unbloody way in the sacrifice of the Mass, and he re-presents the Sacrifice of the Cross and applies its salvific power at the moment when he becomes sacramentally present — through the words of consecration — as the spiritual food of the faithful under the appearances of bread and wine.

Various Ways in Which Christ Is Present

35. All of us realize that there is more than one way in which Christ is present in his Church. We want to go into this very joyful subject, which the Constitution on the Sacred Liturgy presented briefly,[30] at somewhat greater length. Christ is present in his Church when she prays, since he is the one who "prays for us and prays in us and to whom we pray: He prays for us as our priest, he prays in us as our head, he is prayed to by us as our God"[31]; and he is the one who has promised, "Where two or three are gathered together in my name,

I am there in the midst of them."[32] He is present in the Church as she performs her works of mercy, not just because whatever good we do to one of his least brethren we do to Christ himself,[33] but also because Christ is the one who performs these works through the Church and who continually helps men with his divine love. He is present in the Church as she moves along on her pilgrimage with a longing to reach the portals of eternal life, for he is the one who dwells in our hearts through faith,[34] and who instills charity in them through the Holy Spirit whom he gives to us.[35]

36. In still another very genuine way, he is present in the Church as she preaches, since the Gospel which she proclaims is the word of God, and it is only in the name of Christ, the Incarnate Word of God, and by his authority and with his help that it is preached, so that there might be "one flock resting secure in one shepherd."[36]

37. He is present in his Church as she rules and governs the People of God, since her sacred power comes from Christ and since Christ, the "Shepherd of Shep-

herds,"[37] is present in the bishops who exercise that power, in keeping with the promise he made to the apostles.

38. Moreover, Christ is present in his Church in a still more sublime manner as she offers the sacrifice of the Mass in his name; he is present in her as she administers the sacraments. On the matter of Christ's presence in the offering of the sacrifice of the Mass, we would like very much to call what St. John Chrysostom, overcome with awe, had to say in such accurate and eloquent words: "I wish to add something that is clearly awe-inspiring, but do not be surprised or upset. What is this? It is the same offering, no matter who offers it, be it Peter or Paul. It is the same one that Christ gave to his disciples and the same one that priests now perform: The latter is in no way inferior to the former, for it is not men who sanctify the latter, but he who sanctified the former. For just as the words which God spoke are the same as those that the priest now pronounces, so, too, the offering is the same."[38] No one is unaware that the sacraments are the actions of Christ who administers them through

men. And so the sacraments are holy in themselves, and they pour grace into the soul by the power of Christ, when they touch the body: the highest kind of Presence.

These various ways in which Christ is present fill the mind with astonishment and offer the Church a mystery for her contemplation. But there is another way in which Christ is present in his Church, a way that surpasses all the others. It is his presence in the Sacrament of the Eucharist, which is, for this reason, "a more consoling source of devotion, a lovelier object of contemplation and holier in what it contains"[39] than all the other sacraments; for it contains Christ himself and it is "a kind of consummation of the spiritual life, and in a sense the goal of all the sacraments."[40]

39. This presence is called "real" not to exclude the idea that the others are "real," too, but rather to indicate presence par excellence, because it is substantial and through it Christ becomes present whole and entire, God and man.[41] And so it would be wrong for anyone to try to ex-

plain this manner of presence by dreaming up a so-called pneumatic nature of the glorious body of Christ that would be present everywhere; or for anyone to limit it to symbolism, as if this most sacred Sacrament were to consist in nothing more than an efficacious sign "of the spiritual presence of Christ and of his intimate union with the faithful, the members of his Mystical Body."[42]

The Proper Use of Symbolism

40. It is true that the Fathers and Scholastics had a great deal to say about symbolism in the Eucharist, especially with regard to the unity of the Church. The Council of Trent, in restating their doctrine, taught that our Savior bequeathed the Eucharist to his Church "as a symbol ... of the unity and charity with which he wished all Christians to be joined among themselves," "and hence as a symbol of that one Body of which he is the head."[43]

41. When Christian literature was still in its infancy, the unknown author of the work called the "Didache," or "Teaching of the Twelve Apostles," had this to write on the subject: "As far as the Eucharist

is concerned, give thanks in this manner: ... just as this bread had been broken and scattered over the hills and was made one when it was gathered together, so, too, may your church be gathered into your kingdom from the ends of the earth."[44]

42. St. Cyprian, too, in the course of laying stress on the Church's unity in opposition to schism, said this: "Finally the Lord's sacrifices proclaim the unity of Christians who are bound together by a firm and unshakable charity. For when the Lord calls the bread that has been made from many grains of wheat his body, he is describing our people whose unity he has sustained; and when he refers to wine pressed from many grapes and berries as his blood, once again he is speaking of our flock which has been formed by fusing many into one."[45]

43. But before all of these, St. Paul had written to the Corinthians: "The one bread makes us one body, though we are many in number; the same bread is shared by all."[46]

Symbolism Inadequate to Express Real Presence

44. While Eucharistic symbolism is well suited to helping us understand the effect that is proper to this Sacrament — the unity of the Mystical Body — still it does not indicate or explain what it is that makes this Sacrament different from all the others. For the constant teaching that the Catholic Church has passed on to her catechumens, the understanding of the Christian people, the doctrine defined by the Council of Trent, the very words that Christ used when he instituted the most holy Eucharist, all require us to profess that "the Eucharist is the flesh of our Savior Jesus Christ which suffered for our sins and which the Father in his loving kindness raised again."[47] To these words of St. Ignatius we may well add those which Theodore of Mopsuestia, who is a faithful witness to the faith of the Church on this point, addressed to the people: "The Lord did not say: This is symbol of my body, and this is a symbol of my blood, but rather: This is my body and my blood. He teaches us not to look to the nature of what lies before us and is perceived by the senses, because the giving of thanks and

the words spoken over it have changed it into flesh and blood."[48]

45. The Council of Trent, basing itself on this faith of the Church, "openly and sincerely professes that after the consecration of the bread and wine, our Lord Jesus Christ, true God and man, is really, truly and substantially contained in the Blessed Sacrament of the holy Eucharist under the outward appearances of sensible things." And so our Savior is present in his humanity, not only in his natural manner of existence at the right hand of the Father, but also at the same time in the Sacrament of the Eucharist "in a manner of existing that we can hardly express in words but that our minds, illumined by faith, can come to see as possible to God and that we must most firmly believe."[49]

CHRIST PRESENT IN THE EUCHARIST THROUGH TRANSUBSTANTIATION

46. To avoid any misunderstanding of this type of presence, which goes beyond the laws of nature and constitutes the greatest miracle of its kind,[50] we have to listen with docility to the voice of the teaching

and praying Church. Her voice, which constantly echoes the voice of Christ, assures us that the way in which Christ becomes present in this Sacrament is through the conversion of the whole substance of the bread into his body and of the whole substance of the wine into his blood, a unique and truly wonderful conversion that the Catholic Church fittingly and properly calls transubstantiation.[51] As a result of transubstantiation, the species of bread and wine undoubtedly take on a new signification and a new finality, for they are no longer ordinary bread and wine but instead a sign of something sacred and a sign of spiritual food; but they take on this new signification, this new finality, precisely because they contain a new "reality" which we can rightly call ontological. For what now lies beneath the aforementioned species is not what was there before, but something completely different; and not just in the estimation of Church belief but in reality, since once the substance or nature of the bread and wine has been changed into the body and blood of Christ, nothing remains of the bread and the wine except for the species — beneath which Christ is present whole and entire in his physical "reality," corporeally present, although not in the manner in which bodies are in a place.

Writings of the Fathers

47. This is why the Fathers felt they had a solemn duty to warn the faithful that, in reflecting upon this most sacred Sacrament, they should not pay attention to the senses, which report only the properties of bread and wine, but rather to the words of Christ, which have power great enough to change, transform, "transelementize" the bread and wine into his body and blood. As a matter of fact, as the same Fathers point out on more than one occasion, the power that does this is the same power of Almighty God that created the whole universe out of nothing at the beginning of time.

48. "Instructed as you are in these matters," says St. Cyril of Jerusalem, at the end of a sermon on the mysteries of the Faith, "and filled with an unshakable faith that what seems to be bread is not bread — though it tastes like it — but rather the body of Christ; and that what seems to be wine is not wine — even though it

too tastes like it — but rather the Blood of Christ … draw strength from receiving this bread as spiritual food and your soul will rejoice."[52]

49. St. John Chrysostom insists upon the same point with these words: "It is not man who makes what is put before him the body and blood of Christ, but Christ himself who was crucified for us. The priest standing there in the place of Christ says these words, but their power and grace are from God. This is my body, he says, and these words transform what lies before him."[53]

50. Cyril, the bishop of Alexandria, is in wonderful harmony with John, the bishop of Constantinople, when he writes in his commentary on the Gospel of St. Matthew: "He said this is my body and this is my blood in a demonstrative fashion, so that you might not judge that what you see is a mere figure; instead the offerings are truly changed by the hidden power of God Almighty into Christ's body and blood, which bring us the life-giving and sanctifying power of Christ when we share in them."[54]

51. Ambrose, the bishop of Milan, in a clear statement on the Eucharistic conversion, has this to say: "Let us be assured that this is not what nature formed but what the blessing has consecrated; and there is greater power in the blessing and in nature, since nature itself is changed through the blessing." To confirm the truth of this mystery, he recounts many of the miracles described in the Sacred Scriptures, including Christ's birth of the Virgin Mary, and then he turns his mind to the work of creation, concluding this way: "Surely the word of Christ, who could make something that did not exist out of nothing, can change things that do exist into something they were not before. For it is no less extraordinary to give new natures to things than it is to change nature."[55]

Constant Teaching of the Popes and the Councils

52. But this is no time for assembling a long list of evidence. Instead, we would rather recall the firmness of faith and complete unanimity that the Church displayed in opposing Berengarius [of Tours] who gave in to certain difficulties raised

by human reasoning and first dared to deny the Eucharistic conversion. More than once [the Church] threatened to condemn him unless he retracted. Thus it was that our predecessor St. Gregory VII [who] commanded him to swear to the following oath: "I believe in my heart and openly profess that the bread and wine that are placed on the altar are, through the mystery of the sacred prayer and the words of the Redeemer, substantially changed into the true and proper and life-giving flesh and blood of Jesus Christ our Lord, and that after the consecration they are the true body of Christ — which was born of the Virgin and which hung on the cross as an offering for the salvation of the world — and the true blood of Christ — which flowed from his side — and not just as a sign and by reason of the power of the Sacrament, but in the very truth and reality of their substance and in what is proper to their nature."[56]

53. We have a wonderful example of the stability of the Catholic faith in the way in which these words meet with such complete agreement in the constant teaching of the Ecumenical Councils of Lateran,

Constance, Florence, and Trent on the mystery of the Eucharistic conversion, whether it be contained in their explanations of the teaching of the Church or in their condemnations of error.

54. After the Council of Trent, our predecessor Pius VI issued a serious warning, on the occasion of the errors of the Synod of Pistoia, that parish priests not neglect to speak of transubstantiation, which is listed among the articles of the Faith, in the course of carrying out their office of teaching.[57] Similarly, our predecessor of happy memory, Pius XII, recalled the bounds beyond which those who were carrying on subtle discussion of the mystery of transubstantiation might not pass;[58] and we ourself, at the National Eucharistic Congress that was recently celebrated at Pisa, bore open and solemn witness to the faith of the Church, in fulfillment of our apostolic duty.[59]

55. Moreover, the Catholic Church has held firm to this belief in the presence of Christ's body and blood in the Eucharist not only in her teaching but in her life as well, since she has at all times paid

this great Sacrament the worship known as "latria," which may be given to God alone. As St. Augustine says, "It was in his flesh that Christ walked among us and it is his flesh that he has given us to eat for our salvation; but no one eats of this flesh without having first adored it ... and not only do we not sin in thus adoring it, but we would be sinning if we did not do so."[60]

ON THE WORSHIP OF LATRIA

56. The Catholic Church has always displayed and still displays this latria that ought to be paid to the Sacrament of the Eucharist, both during Mass and outside of it, by taking the greatest possible care of consecrated Hosts, by exposing them to the solemn veneration of the faithful, and by carrying them about in processions to the joy of great numbers of the people.

57. The ancient documents of the Church offer many evidences of this veneration. The bishops of the Church always urged the faithful to take the greatest possible care of the Eucharist that they had in their homes. "The Body of Christ is meant to be eaten by the faithful, not to be treated

with irreverence" is the serious warning of St. Hippolytus.[61]

58. In fact, the faithful regarded themselves as guilty, and rightly so as Origen recalls, if, after they had received the body of the Lord and kept it with all reverence and caution, some part of it were to fall to the ground through negligence.[62]

59. These same bishops were severe in reproving any lack of due reverence that might occur. We have evidence of this from the words of Novatian, whose testimony is trustworthy in this matter; he felt that anybody deserved to be condemned who "came out after Sunday service bringing the Eucharist with him, as was the custom … and carried the holy body of the Lord around with him," going off to places of amusement instead of going home.[63]

60. In fact, St. Cyril of Alexandria denounced as mad the opinion that the Eucharist was of no use to sanctification if some of it were left over for another day. "For Christ is not altered," he says, "and his holy body is not changed; instead the power and force and life-giving grace of

the blessing remain in it forever."[64]

61. Nor should we forget that in ancient times the faithful — whether being harassed by violent persecutions or living in solitude out of love for monastic life — nourished themselves, even daily on the Eucharist, by receiving holy Communion from their own hands when there was no priest or deacon present.[65]

62. We are not saying this with any thought of effecting a change in the manner of keeping the Eucharist and of receiving holy Communion that has been laid down by subsequent ecclesiastical laws still in force; our intention is that we may rejoice over the faith of the Church which is always one and the same.

Corpus Christi, Another Instance of Latria

63. This faith also gave rise to the feast of Corpus Christi, which was first celebrated in the Diocese of Liege — especially through the efforts of the servant of God Blessed Juliana of Mount Cornelius — and our predecessor Urban IV, established for the universal Church. It has

also given rise to many forms of Eucharistic devotion that have, through the inspiration of God's grace, grown with each passing day. Through them the Catholic Church is eagerly striving to pay honor to Christ and to thank him for such a great gift and to beg his mercy.

EXHORTATION TO FOSTERING EUCHARISTIC DEVOTION

64. And so we beseech you, venerable brothers, to take this faith, which means nothing less than maintaining complete fidelity to the words of Christ and the apostles, and preserve it in its purity and integrity among the people entrusted to your care and vigilance, with all false and pernicious opinions being completely rejected; and we beseech you to foster devotion to the Eucharist, which should be the focal point and goal of all other forms of devotion.

65. May the faithful, thanks to your constant efforts, come to realize and experience more and more that: "He who wants to live can find here a place to live in and the means to live on. Let him approach, let him believe, let him be incorporated so

that he may receive life. Let him not shy away from union with the members, let him not be a rotten member that deserves to be cut away, nor a distorted member to be ashamed of. Let him be beautiful, let him be fitting, let him be healthy. Let him adhere to the body; let him live for God on God: Let him labor now upon earth, so that he may afterwards reign in heaven."[66]

Daily Mass and Holy Communion

66. It is desirable to have the faithful in large numbers take an active part in the sacrifice of the Mass each and every day and receive the nourishment of holy Communion with a pure and holy mind and offer fitting thanks to Christ the Lord for such a great gift. They should remember these words: "The desire of Jesus Christ and of the Church to see all the faithful approach the sacred banquet each and every day is based on a wish to have them all united to God through the Sacrament and to have them draw from it the strength to master their passions, to wash away the lesser sins that are committed every day, and to prevent the serious sins to which human frailty is subject."[67] And they should not forget about paying a visit

during the day to the most blessed Sacrament in the very special place of honor where it is reserved in churches in keeping with the liturgical laws, since this is a proof of gratitude and a pledge of love and a display of the adoration that is owed to Christ the Lord who is present there.

Dignity Bestowed by Eucharist

67. No one can fail to see that the divine Eucharist bestows an incomparable dignity upon the Christian people. For it is not just while the Sacrifice is being offered and the Sacrament is being confected, but also after the Sacrifice has been offered and the Sacrament confected — while the Eucharist is reserved in churches or oratories — that Christ is truly Emmanuel, which means "God with us." For he is in the midst of us day and night; he dwells in us with the fullness of grace and of truth.[68] He raises the level of morals, fosters virtue, comforts the sorrowful, strengthens the weak, and stirs up all those who draw near to him to imitate him, so that they may learn from his example to be meek and humble of heart and to seek not their own interests but those of God. Anyone who has a special devotion to the sacred

Eucharist and who tries to repay Christ's infinite love for us with an eager and unselfish love of his own will experience and fully understand — and this will bring great delight and benefit to his soul — just how precious is a life hidden with Christ in God,[69] and just how worthwhile it is to carry on a conversation with Christ, for there is nothing more consoling here on earth, nothing more efficacious for progress along the paths of holiness.

68. You also realize, venerable brothers, that the Eucharist is reserved in churches or oratories to serve as the spiritual center of a religious community or a parish community, indeed of the whole Church and the whole of mankind, since it contains, beneath the veil of the species, Christ the invisible head of the Church, the Redeemer of the world, the center of all hearts, "by whom all things are and by whom we exist."[70]

69. Hence it is that devotion to the divine Eucharist exerts a great influence upon the soul in the direction of fostering a "social" love,[71] in which we put the common good ahead of private good, take up the

cause of the community, the parish, the universal Church, and extend our charity to the whole world because we know that there are members of Christ everywhere.

A Sign and Cause of Unity

70. Because, venerable brothers, the Sacrament of the Eucharist is a sign and cause of the unity of Christ's Mystical Body, and because it stirs up an active "ecclesial" spirit in those who are more fervent in their Eucharistic devotion, never stop urging your faithful, as they approach the Mystery of the Eucharist, to learn to embrace the Church's cause as their own, to pray to God without slackening, to offer themselves to God as an acceptable sacrifice for the peace and unity of the Church; so that all the sons of the Church may be united and feel united and there may be no divisions among them but rather unity of mind and intention, as the apostle commands.[72] May all those who are not yet in perfect communion with the Catholic Church and who glory in the name of Christian despite their separation from her, come as soon as possible to share with us, through the help of God's grace, in that unity of faith and commu-

nion that Christ wanted to be the distinctive mark of his disciples.

A Special Task for Religious

71. This zeal at prayer and at devoting oneself to God for the sake of the unity of the Church is something that religious, both men and women, should regard as very specially their own since they are bound in a special way to adoration of the Blessed Sacrament, and they have, by virtue of the vows they have pronounced, become a kind of crown set around it here on earth.

The Tridentine Decree

72. The Church in the past has felt and still feels that nothing is more ancient and more pleasing than the desire for the unity of all Christians, and we want to express this in the very same words that the Council of Trent used to conclude its decree on the most holy Eucharist: "In conclusion, the council with paternal love admonishes, exhorts, begs, and implores through the merciful kindness of our God[73] that each and every Christian may come at last to full agreement in this sign of unity, in this bond of charity, in this symbol of harmony; that they may be mindful of the great

dignity and the profound love of Our Lord, Jesus Christ, who gave up his precious life as the price of our salvation and who gave us his flesh to eat;[74] and that they may believe and adore these sacred mysteries of his body and blood with such firm and unwavering faith, with such devotion and piety and veneration, that they will be able to receive that supersubstantial[75] bread often, and it will truly be the life of their souls and the unfailing strength of their minds, so that, 'fortified by its vigor,'[76] they may be able to move on from this wretched earthly pilgrimage to their heavenly home where, without any veil, they will eat the 'bread of angels'[77] that they now eat beneath the sacred veils."[78]

73. May the all-merciful Redeemer, who shortly before his death prayed to the Father that all who were to believe in him might be one, just as he and the Father are one,[79] deign to hear this most ardent prayer of ours and of the whole Church as quickly as possible, so that we may all celebrate the Eucharistic Mystery with one voice and one faith, and through sharing in the body of Christ become one body,[80] joined together by the same bonds that

Christ wanted it to have.

A Word to the Eastern Churches

74. We also want to address with fraternal affection those who belong to the venerable Churches of the East, which have had so many glorious Fathers whose testimony to belief in the Eucharist we have been so glad to cite in this present letter of ours. Our soul is filled with great joy as we contemplate your belief in the Eucharist, which is ours as well, as we listen to the liturgical prayers you use to celebrate this great mystery, as we behold your Eucharistic devotion, as we read your theological works explaining or defending the doctrine of this most sacred Sacrament.

A Final Prayer

75. May the most blessed Virgin Mary, from whom Christ the Lord took the flesh that "is contained, offered, received"[81] in this Sacrament under the appearances of bread and wine, and may all the saints of God and especially those who were more inflamed with ardent devotion toward the divine Eucharist, intercede with the Father of mercies so that this common belief in the Eucharist and devotion to it

may give rise among all Christians to a perfect unity of communion that will continue to flourish. Lingering in our mind are the words of the holy martyr Ignatius warning the Philadelphians against the evil of divisions and schisms, the remedy for which is to be found in the Eucharist. "Strive then," he says, "to make use of one single thanksgiving. For there is only one flesh of Our Lord, Jesus Christ, and only one chalice unto the union of his blood, only one altar, only one bishop …"[82]

76. Fortified by the most consoling hope of blessings that will accrue to the whole Church and to the whole world from an increase in devotion to the Eucharist, as a pledge of heavenly blessings we lovingly impart our apostolic blessings to you, venerable brothers, and to the priests, religious, and all who are helping you, as well as to all the faithful entrusted to your care.

Given at St. Peter's, Rome, on the third day of September, the feast of Pope St. Pius X, in the year 1965, the third of our pontificate.

PAUL VI

NOTES

LATIN TEXT: *Acta Apostolicae Sedis*, 57 (1965), 753–74.

ENGLISH TRANSLATION: *The Pope Speaks*, 10 (Fall, 1965), 309–28.

REFERENCES:

1. *Constitution on the Sacred Liturgy*, c. 2, n. 47: AAS LVI (1964), 113 [Cf. TPS IX, 325.].
2. Jn 6:55.
3. Cf. Jn 17:23.
4. Encyclical letter *Mirae caritatis*: *Acta Leonis XIII*, XXII (1902–1903), 122.
5. *Homily on Matthew*, 82.4; PG 58.743.
6. *Summa Theologiae* III,(a) q. 75, a. 1, c.
7. *In IV Sent., dist.* X, P. I, art. un., qu. I; *Opera omnia, tome* IV, Ad Claras Aquas (1889), 217.
8. Jn 6:61–69.
9. St. Augustine, *Against Julian*, VI, 5.11; PL 44.829.
10. *City of God*, X, 23; PL 41.300.
11. *Dogmatic Constitution on the Catholic Faith*, c. 4.
12. Cf. Council of Trent, *Teaching on the Holy Sacrifice of the Mass*, c. I.
13. Cf. Ex 24:8.
14. Lk 22:19–20; cf. Mt 26:26–28; Mk 14:22–24.
15. Acts 2:42.
16. Acts 4:32.
17. 1 Cor 11:23ff.
18. 1 Cor 10:16.
19. Cf. Mal 1:11.
20. Council of Trent, *Doctrine on the Holy Sacrifice of the Mass*, c. 2.
21. *Catecheses*, 23 [*myst.* 5]. 8–18; PG 33.1115–1118.
22. Cf. *Confessions* IX, 12.32; PL 32.777; cf. ibid. IX 11, 27; PL 32.775.

NOTES

23. Cf. *Sermon* 172.2.; PL 38.936; cf. *On the care to be taken of the dead*, 13, PL 40.593.

24. Cf. St. Augustine, *City of God*, X, 6; PL 42.284.

25. Cf. Encyclical letter *Mediator Dei*; AAS XXXIX (1947), 552.

26. Cf. *Dogmatic Constitution on the Church*, c. 2, 11; AAS LVII (1965), 15 [cf. TPS v. 10, p. 366].

27. Cf. ibid., c. 2, n. 10; AAS LVII (1965), 14 [Cf. TPS v. 10, p. 365–366.].

28. *Constitution on the Sacred Liturgy*, c. 1, n. 27; AAS LVI (1964), 107 [cf. TPS IX, 322].

29. Cf. Roman Pontifical.

30. Cf. c. 1, n. 7; AAS LVI (1964), 100–101.

31. St. Augustine, *On Psalm* 85.1: PL 37.1081.

32. Mt 18:20.

33. Cf. Mt 25:40.

34. Cf. Eph 3:17.

35. Cf. Rom 5:5.

36. St. Augustine, *Against the Letter of Petiliani*, III, 10.11; PL 43.353.

37. St. Augustine, *On Psalm* 86.3; PL 37.1102.

38. *Homily on the Second Epistle to Timothy* 2.4; PG 62.612.

39. Giles of Rome, *Theorems on the Body of Christ*, theor. 50 (Venice, 1521), p. 127.

40. St. Thomas, *Summa Theologiae,* IIIa, p. 73, a. 3, c.

41. Cf. Council of Trent, *Decree on the Holy Eucharist*, c. 3.

42. Pius XII, Encyclical letter *Humani generis*: AAS XLII (1950), 578.

43. *Decree on the Holy Eucharist*, Introduction and c. 2.

44. Didache, 9.1; F. X. Funk, *Patres Apostolici*, 1.20.

45. *Epistle to Magnus*, 6; PL 3.1139.

46. 1 Cor 10:17.

47. St. Ignatius, *Epistle to the Smyrnians*, 7.1; PG 5.714.

48. *Commentary on Matthew*, c. 26; PG 66.714.

49. *Decree on the Holy Eucharist*, c. 1.

50. Cf. *Mirae caritatis*; *Acta Leonis XIII*, XXII (1902–1903), 123.

51 Cf. *Decree on the Holy Eucharist*, c. 4 and canon 2.

52. *Catecheses*, 22.9 [*myst.* 4] PG 33.1103.

53. *Homily on Judas' betrayal*, 1.6; PG 49.380; cf. Homily on Matthew 82.5; PG 58.744.

54 .*On Matthew* 26.27; PG 72.451.

55. *On Mysteries* 9.50–52; PL 16.422–424.

56 Gian Domenico Mansi, *Collectio amplissima Conciliorum*, XX, 524D.

57. Apostolic constitution *Auctorem fidei*, August 28, 1794.

58. Allocution of September 22, 1956: AAS XLVIII (1956), 720 [cf. TPS III, 281–282].

59. AAS LVII (1965), 588–592.

60. *On Psalm* 98.9; PL 37.1264.

61. *Apostolic Tradition*; ed. Botte, *La Tradition Apostolique de St. Hippolyte*, Muenster (1963), p. 84.

62. *Fragment on Exodus*; PG 12.391.

63. *On Shows*; CSEL III, (3) 8.

64. *Epistle to Calosyrius*; PG 76.1075.

65. Cf. Basil, *Epistle* 93; PG 32.483–486.

66. St. Augustine, *Treatise on John* 26.13; PL 35.1613.

67. Decree of the Sacred Congregation of the Council, December 20, 1905, approved by St. Pius X: AAS XXXVIII (1905), 401.

68. Cf. Jn 1:14.

69. Cf. Col 3:3.

70. 1 Cor 8:6.

71. Cf. St. Augustine, *On the literal interpretation of Genesis* XI, 15.20; PL 34.437.

72. Cf. 1 Cor 1:10.

73. Lk 1:78.

74. Jn 6:48ff.

75. Mt 6:11.

76. 1 Kgs 19:8.

77. Ps 77:25.

78. *Decree on the Holy Eucharist*, c. 8.

79. Cf. Jn 17:20–21.

80. Cf. 1 Cor 10:17.

81. C.I.C., canon 801.

82. *Epistle to the Philadelphians* 4; PG 5.700.